THE SCIENCE OF FAIRY TALES

A Tiny Vegetable Many Mattresses

AND THE SCIENCE OF the Princess AND THE Pea

WRITTEN BY GLORIA KOSTER
ILLUSTRATED BY DUSAN PAVLIC

PICTURE WINDOW BOOKS
a capstone imprint

The Scientific Method

1. Ask a Question

Ask yourself, "What do I want to learn more about?" or "I wonder what would happen if . . . ?"

2. Form a Hypothesis

Make a prediction or an educated guess about what might happen.

3. Experiment

Test your hypothesis by making a plan and conducting an experiment.

4. Observe and Record

Make careful observations during your experiment and write down what you see.

5. Analyze the Data

Collect and study the results of your data. Was your hypothesis correct?

6. Draw a Conclusion

Make your conclusion and share your results.

This is me and my family. Yes, those are all my older brothers. My parents were so delighted to finally have a girl that they named me Princess. That's my name. Really!

My Family

My brothers quickly learned that I was smart,

handy,

and brave.

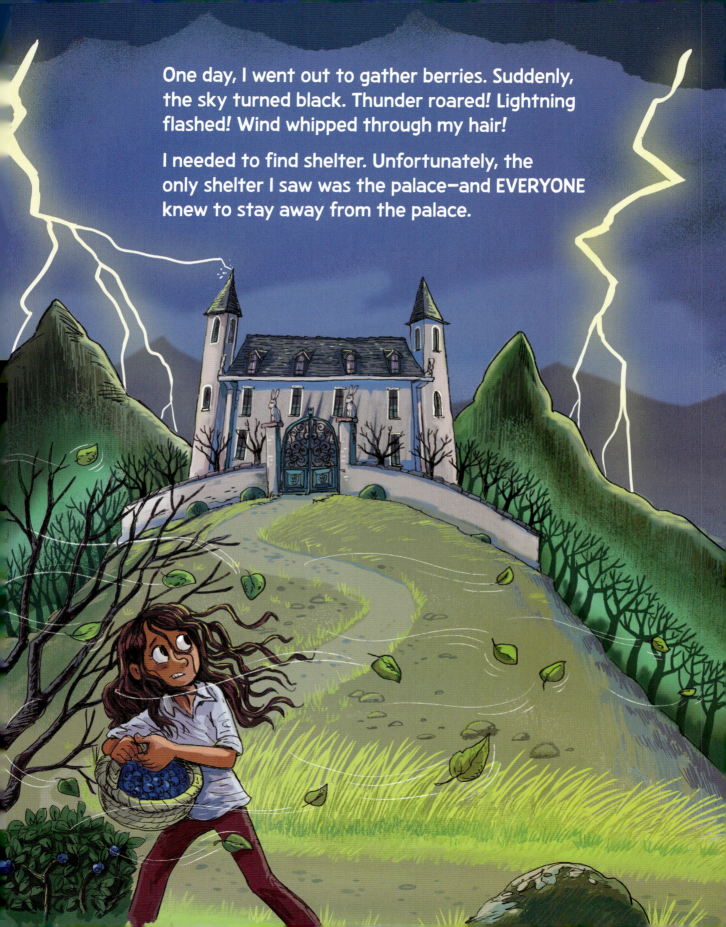

One day, I went out to gather berries. Suddenly, the sky turned black. Thunder roared! Lightning flashed! Wind whipped through my hair!

I needed to find shelter. Unfortunately, the only shelter I saw was the palace—and EVERYONE knew to stay away from the palace.

To my surprise, the Queen answered the door.

"Who are you?" she asked, suspiciously.

"I'm Princess," I answered.

"Princess?" the Queen's eyes lit up. "Come in! You must stay here."

I enjoyed a delicious dinner,

relaxed in a luxurious bath,

and slipped into a proper nightgown.

I was ready for bed, but the bed was quite strange. It had a ladder and 20 mattresses.

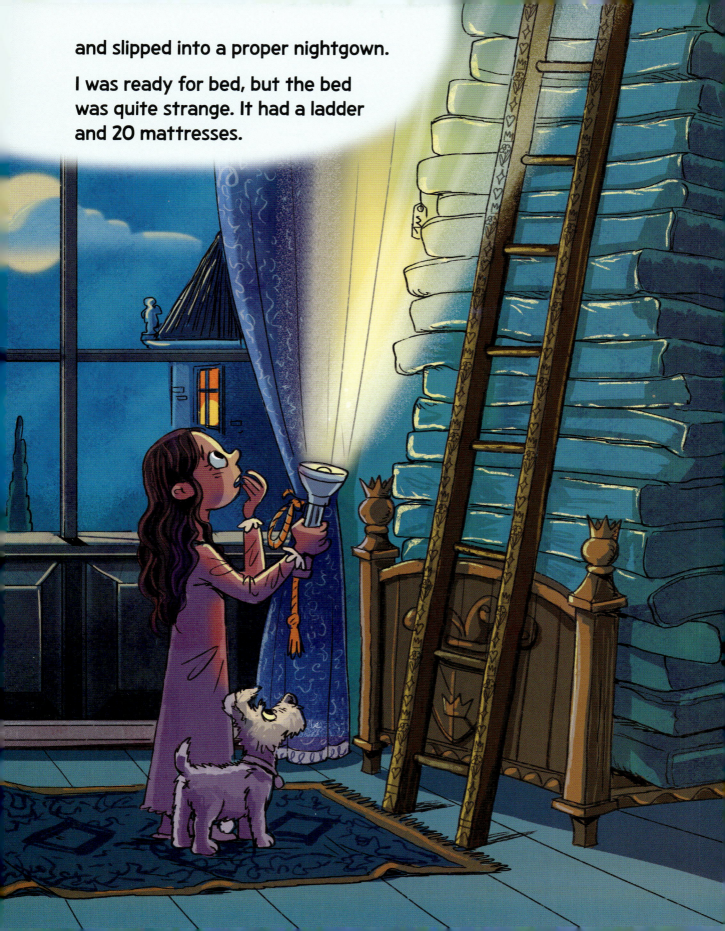

And despite being exhausted, I couldn't sleep at all. I felt like I was lying on stones!

"How did you sleep, Princess?" the Queen asked.

"Terribly," I said. "I felt like I was lying on stones."

"Wonderful news!" said the Queen.

Wonderful? That seemed rude.

"I placed three peas under your mattress," she explained. "Only a true Princess could feel them."

The Prince was smiling from ear to ear.

Flash-forward: The Prince and I fell in love, got married, and had a family. My name was officially Princess Princess.

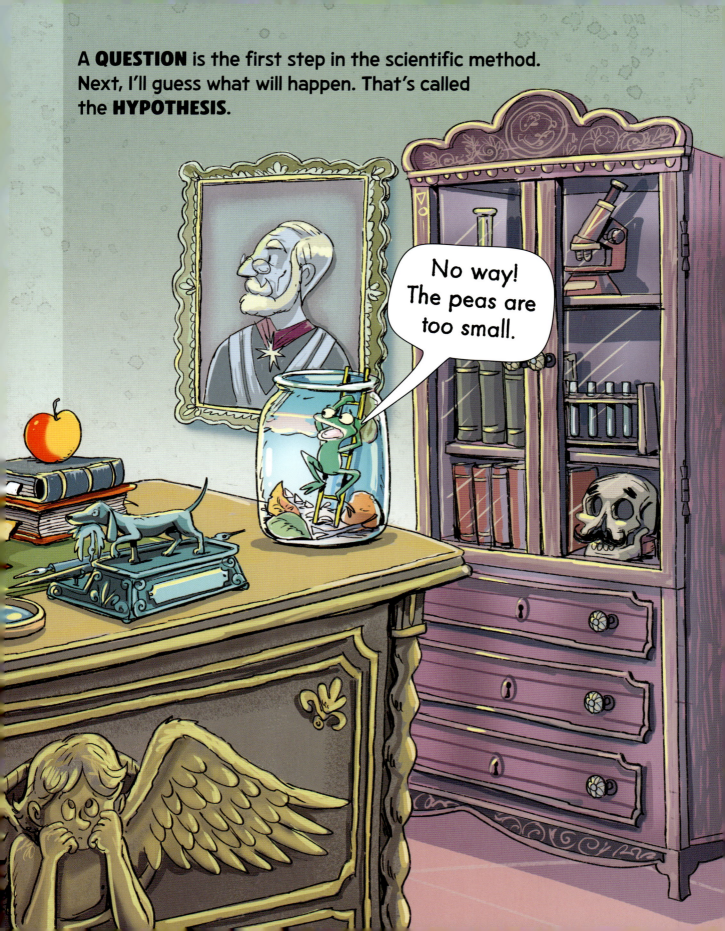

I grab a bag of frozen peas, a thin pillow, a fluffy pillow, and a decorative pillow. Then I get to work!

I take my time and **OBSERVE** my findings as I sit on each pillow. No matter which pillow I tried, I did not feel the peas. Not one little bump.

And I can confidently share my **CONCLUSION**.

So why didn't I sleep? Let's do another experiment to try and find the answer.

QUESTION
Will it take more than 20 paper towel squares to stop feeling a small rock?

HYPOTHESIS
I think it will take more than 20 squares. What's your guess?

EXPERIMENT
Cut paper towels into 20 even squares. Cover the rock one square at a time, lightly pushing down as you go.

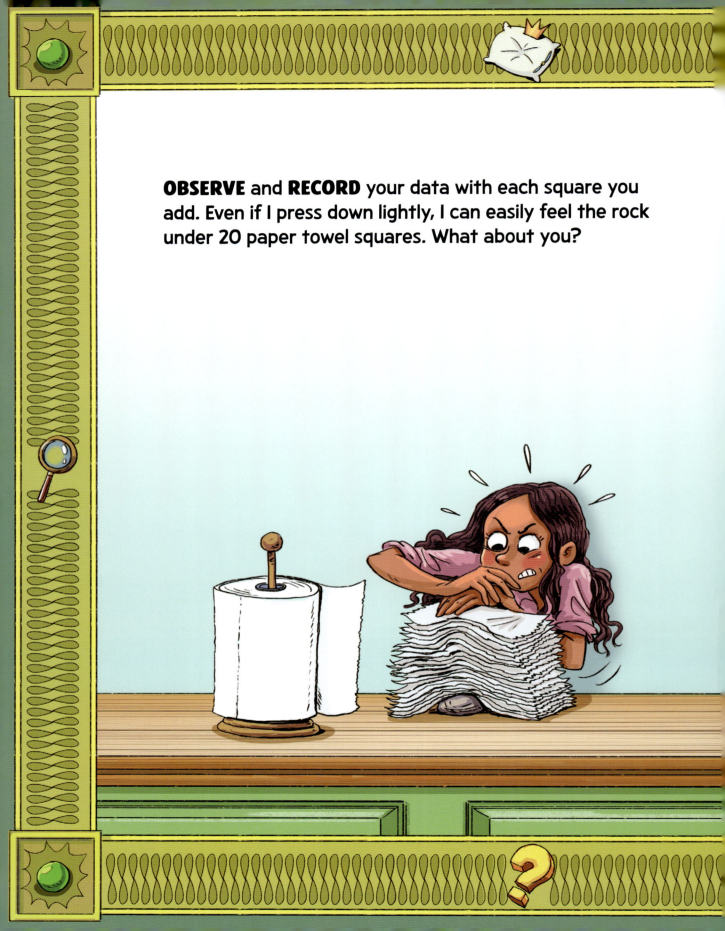

OBSERVE and **RECORD** your data with each square you add. Even if I press down lightly, I can easily feel the rock under 20 paper towel squares. What about you?

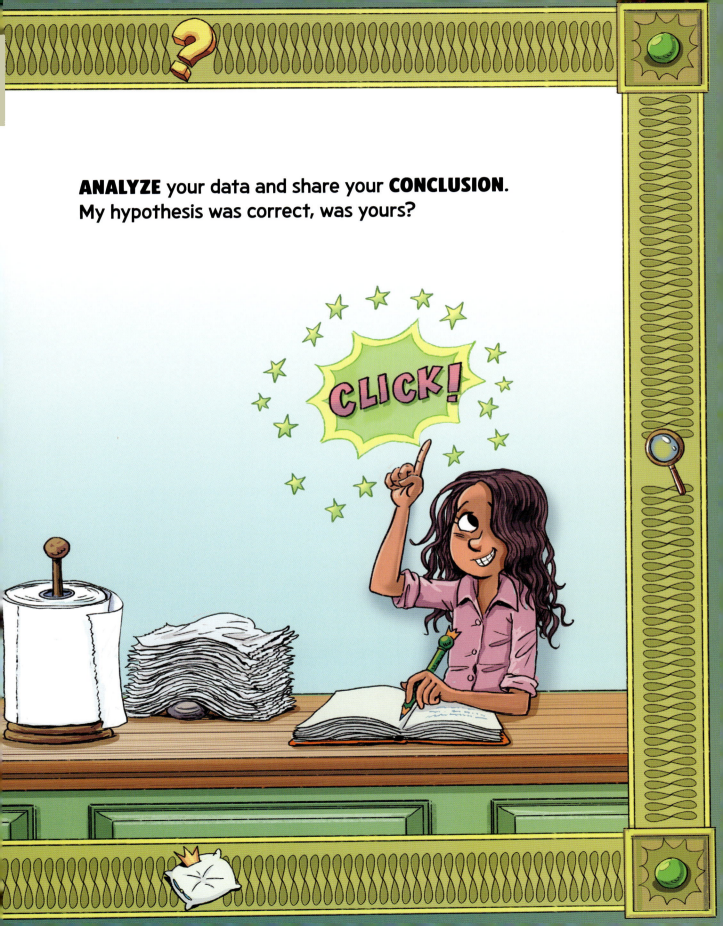

ANALYZE your data and share your **CONCLUSION**. My hypothesis was correct, was yours?

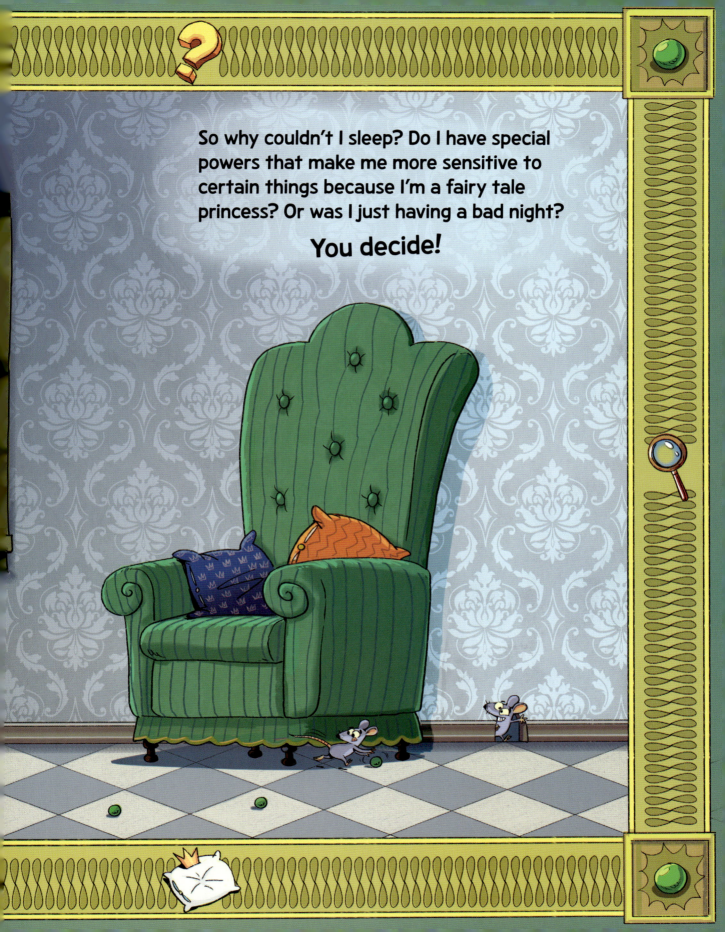

So why couldn't I sleep? Do I have special powers that make me more sensitive to certain things because I'm a fairy tale princess? Or was I just having a bad night?

You decide!

Try Another Experiment

If you still aren't sure, try this experiment focusing on your sense of touch. Touch is how we feel things. But skin may be more sensitive in some places.

QUESTION
Do your hands or arms feel things more?

HYPOTHESIS
Make a guess if your hands or arms feel things more.

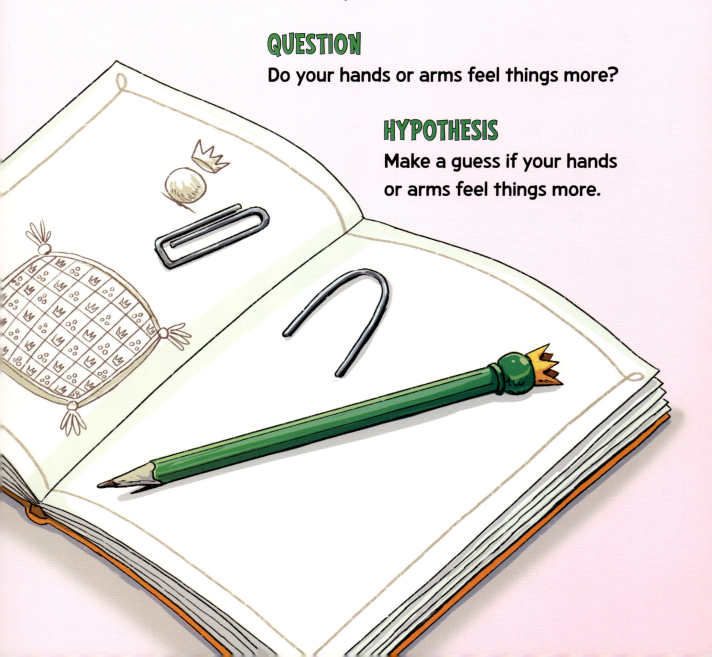

EXPERIMENT

With a partner, use a paper clip to test the feeling in your hands and arms.

1. Unbend a paper clip into a u-shape so there are two points.

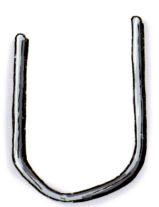

2. Close your eyes as your partner moves the paper clip along your hands and arms.

3. Take a break after each hand and arm to **RECORD** your data. Did you or your partner feel both points at all times? Did it feel the same on both hands and arms?

4. Trade places and repeat the process.

Then **ANALYZE** your data and share your **CONCLUSION**.

Meet the Author

A public and a school librarian, Gloria Koster belongs to the Children's Book Committee of Bank Street College of Education. She enjoys both city and country life, dividing her time between Manhattan and the small town of Pound Ridge, New York. Gloria has three adult children and a bunch of energetic grandkids.

Photo: Miroslav Milić

Meet the Illustrator

Dusan Pavlic has illustrated hundreds of books for publishers around the world. Many of his witty and charming illustrations have won awards, including the Golden Pen. Dusan works as an illustrator and graphic designer in Belgrade, Serbia.

Published by Picture Window Books, an imprint of Capstone
1710 Roe Crest Drive, North Mankato, Minnesota 56003
capstonepub.com

Copyright © 2026 by Capstone. All rights reserved. No part of this publication may be reproduced in whole or in part, or stored in a retrieval system, or transmitted in any form or by any means, electronic, mechanical, photocopying, recording, or otherwise, without written permission of the publisher.

Library of Congress Cataloging-in-Publication Data is available on the Library of Congress website.

ISBN: 9798875216701 (hardcover)
ISBN: 9798875216657 (paperback)
ISBN: 9798875216664 (ebook PDF)

Summary: The story of the Princess and the Pea is retold by Princess, who uses the scientific method to let readers decide if she really felt the pea under all those mattresses.

Editor: Christianne Jones
Designer: Sarah Bennett
Production Specialist: Katy LaVigne

Printed and bound in China. 6274